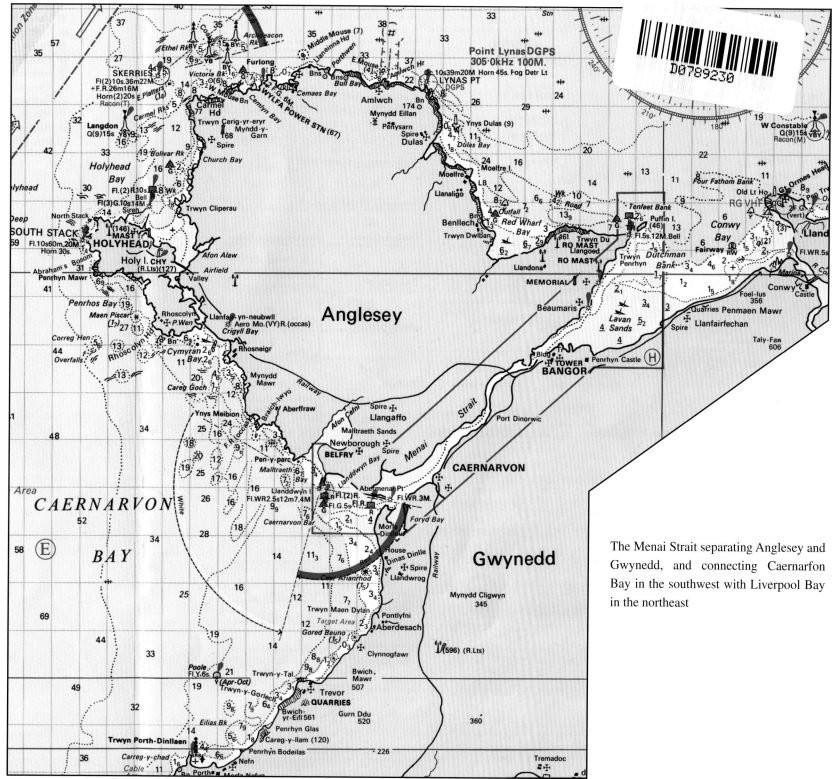

The Menai Strait separating Anglesey and Gwynedd, and connecting Caernarfon Bay in the southwest with Liverpool Bay in the northeast

THE
MENAI
STRAIT

THE MENAI STRAIT

GWYN PARI HUWS

PHOTOGRAPHY: TERRY BEGGS

Llanddwyn old lighthouse from seaward.

GOMER

First Impression – 2003

ISBN 1 84323 333 9 (Hardback)
ISBN 1 84323 271 5 (Paperback)

The publishers wish to acknowledge the permission granted by the Hydrographic Office and Imray to reproduce the naval charts seen in the book and illustrating the end-papers of this volume

Printed in Wales by
Gomer Press, Llandysul, Ceredigion

Preface

In Welsh we say *Y Fenai* – The Menai, (mutation transforming the *M* to *F* following the article *y*) or *Afon Menai*, i.e. The Menai River. It is not really a river of course, rather it is part of the sea; its waters are salt and subject to tidal flow but the many different features along its eighteen-mile length make it a quite spectacular waterway.

While many local inhabitants and visitors to the area are familiar with some aspects of the Strait, comparatively few have had the opportunity to traverse its full length and see the variety and splendour of those features as a sequence. This book is an attempt to provide such a sequence by presenting the Menai Strait in a series of photographs taken from the shoreline or from a boat while following the tideway from west to east.

We commence the passage off Llanddwyn Island at the position which appears in the frontispiece photograph and which is the view from a boat approaching the haven in Llanddwyn's shelter or heading in for the Bar at the western entrance to the Menai itself. Even if you are a armchair sailor, we do hope that you will enjoy following the course of this unique and wonderful waterway.

CONTENTS

FROM LLANDDWYN
TO CAERNARFON

Lighthouse, you say – but where's the lantern?

Three geographical characteristics can make the western entrance to the Menai Strait hazardous for the mariner. The first is that the shores on either side of the estuary are low lying and virtually devoid of useful landmarks by which a ship's position may be ascertained; the second is that the course of the entrance channel through the sandbanks changes from year to year; and the third is the frequently dangerous effect of the prevailing southwesterly winds.

At the northwesterly extremity, however, there is the Llanddwyn promontory, one of the area's few geographical features for which a course may be steered and where a modicum of shelter may be obtained in bad weather. To assist in its recognition from seaward, a white tower was erected in the late eighteenth century and in 1824 a second, larger version was built. There is some uncertainty as to whether the new and larger tower showed a light when it was first erected, but there are records regarding a light from 1846 when the building was modified to include a proper lantern room. Contrary to normal practice, the lantern was sited on the ground floor, as the height of the rock provides sufficient elevation at that position. In the adjacent photograph, the lantern room is the 'extension' that can be seen at the foot of the tower.

The larger tower remains important as a landfall mark for those approaching the Strait from the westward, while the smaller tower carries the current solar-powered light.

When one considers the great number of windmills that operated on Anglesey in days gone by, it is not surprising that the builders followed the same form when they came to build the light towers on Llanddwyn.

Sea and spray at Porth Tŵr Mawr, Llanddwyn.

The meaning of the Welsh word *porth* is closer to the French *porte* than to the English *port,* i.e. essentially an opening. In the marine sense it can indicate anything from a narrow passage between rocks, to a reasonable haven for small craft or, as in this photograph, a small bay – which is certainly an 'opening' but seldom a safe haven! *Tŵr Mawr* is 'Large Tower'.

An idyllic scene looking from Llanddwyn towards Dinas Dinlle over the beach at Porth y Clochydd, and the rocky islet called Ynys y Clochydd.

Clochydd (literally 'bellringer') is the person known in English as the Sexton or perhaps the Verger, and the name suggests an echo from Llanddwyn's ecclesiastical period.

Part of an outcrop of very ancient rock which can be seen at the southern end of Llanddwyn 'island'. Thought to date from some 570 million years ago when it began life as dark ocean-floor volcanic basalt, its characteristics have been completely transformed by natural processes during the intervening ages so that it now displays the pink and cream hues seen in the photograph. A genuine example of the Rock of Ages!

A handsome memorial cross on Llanddwyn which carries a verse of tribute to three local stalwarts who, strangely, are not named! In the background are the ruins of St. Dwynwen's Church.

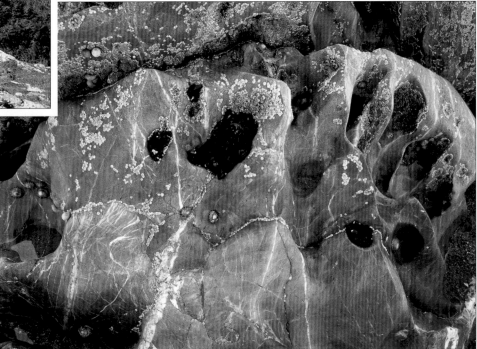

Pilot's Cove, Llanddwyn – a mile's walk along the shore from the nearest car-park, but what a small price to pay for such an enchanting spot!

The cottages were built by the Caernarfon Harbour Trust early in the nineteenth century to house the pilots required to guide vessels into (and out of) the Strait and over the Bar.

These pilots also served as crew for the successive lifeboats stationed at Llanddwyn and, after the light was established on Twr Mawr in 1846, they served as lightkeepers as well as pilots.

A Port Penrhyn-based fishing vessel off Caernarfon Bar, dredging for seed-mussels to transplant to the Lavan Sands at the eastern end of the Menai Strait (see also page 83).

The red *Mussel Bank* buoy about a mile to seaward of the narrow entrance to the Strait at Abermenai. The sea-bed in this vicinity has been renowned for its mussel beds for many generations and was so marked (but spelt *muscle*!) by Lewis Morris on the chart he published in 1748 (chart 3, opposite).

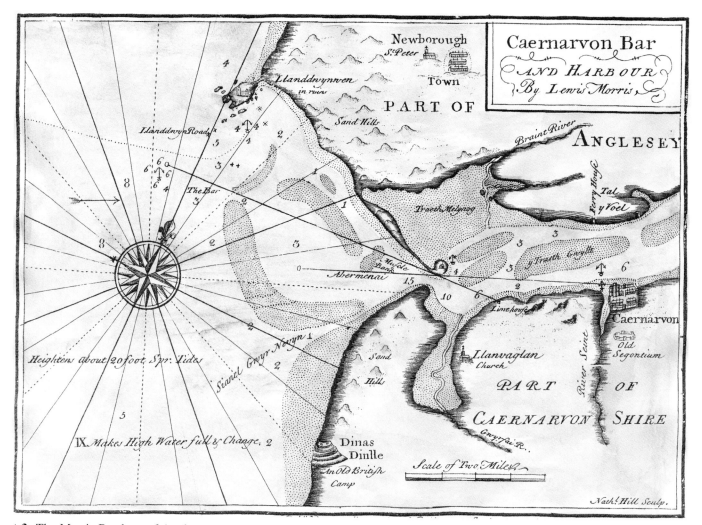

Chart 3: The Morris Brothers of Anglesey (*Morrisiaid Môn*) have long been recognised for their remarkable contribution to, and influence on, the cultural life of Wales during the eighteenth century; the eldest brother Lewis, in particular, would today be described as a polymath. He was a leading Welsh scholar, poet and prolific letter-writer, but also a surveyor of estates, a customs officer, and an inspector of mines. In addition, and most remarkably, he spent a number of years conducting a hydrographic survey of the Welsh coast for the Admiralty. The chart shown here is one of those published by him in 1748 in the volume entitled *Plans of Harbours, Bars, Bays and Roads in St. George's Channel*.

Two items are worthy of particular note. Northwest of Dinas Dinlle will be seen the words *Sianel Gwyr Nevyn* – 'The Nevyn Men's Channel'; avoiding the Bar, it affords the shortest passage from Nefyn to Caernarfon, and is still used today by those with good local knowledge. Bottom left is the legend *IX Makes High Water full & Change* – which indicates that high water occurs at 9 o'clock on the days of full and new moon. This matter will be discussed later in the book.

Looking towards the Llŷn peninsula from the dunes between Llanddwyn and Abermenai.
The three peaks of the Rivals (Yr Eifl) are clear, as also is Garn Fadryn in the distance.

Passing here by boat in a southeasterly direction, one is conscious that the shores of Anglesey and Arfon are rapidly closing to form the narrows at Abermenai.

Abermenai sand-dune sculpted by the wind, and the Marram grass that provides stability.

Dune Pansy (*Viola Tricolor*) in its natural habitat.

The Norman French, led by Edward I – who suppressed North Wales in the thirteenth century and raised the huge castles – came from the eastward, by land; the later French threat in the eighteenth century was of an invasion from the sea, in the opposite direction.

It was primarily this concern which led Lord Newborough to develop a fort to defend the southwesterly entrance to the Strait. Known as Abermenai Barracks when it was first established in the late eighteenth century, it had assumed its present form and structure by about 1840, and had been re-named Belan Fort.

Though the original threat from the French (and from American privateers during the War of Independence) had long since vanished by the time the fort had been completed, it remained an ideal position from which to defend the Strait from seaborne attack, and was manned and armed for that purpose during the Second World War.

Harebells, *Campanula Rotundifolia* growing beneath the muzzles of the guns.

Belan Fort, one of the corner towers.

The inner portico and sundial.

The sundial indicates natural time by the sun i.e. *local apparent time*. To obtain Greenwich time, the time shown by the dial must be increased by about 17 minutes to allow for the site's westerly longitude and also corrected for the *equation of time*. This is an adjustment varying with the date, for the earth's irregular movement in orbit around the sun. A framed table combining the two elements was amongst the contents of the fort which were transferred to the care of the Liverpool Maritime Museum in 1986.

The dock at Belan, looking to the southeast, with Snowdon in the distance.

Abermenai lightbeacon. To the mariner inward bound to the Strait, the beacon shows a white light in an arc over the channel and a red arc over the shoal water. By keeping within the white arc, a craft should enter the Strait safely.

It was from here that the Abermenai Ferry crossed between Anglesey and the mainland for hundreds of years until the middle of the nineteenth century. Yachtsmen familiar with the strong tidal stream through the narrows will wonder how a ferryman could maintain a regular service across it – or perhaps any regularity was in accordance with the hours of minimum tidal flow, around slack water.

The ruin in the background was at one time the powder magazine to which explosives destined for the local slate quarries were transferred from ships, which anchored at Abermenai for the purpose.

The lightbeacon can be seen again on the left, and the passenger boat *Queen of the Sea turning* off the point for the return passage to the quay at Caernarfon. In common parlance, incidentally, the narrows at Abermenai are known as the *gap* – in Welsh as well as in English!

Abermenai anchorage at low water on a summer's afternoon, with Caernarfon in the background.

In earlier times small sailing vessels used this anchorage, which benefits from some shelter provided by the dunes on the point. It was also used by the ships bringing in the explosives mentioned previously. Though sheltered from the prevailing winds, vigilance is still required as the tide, particularly the ebb, flows strongly through the anchorage. Beyond the yachts is a tongue of the bank known as Traeth Melynog. *Traeth* is commonly the word for 'beach' but in this context means 'bank', while *melynog* means 'yellowy'.

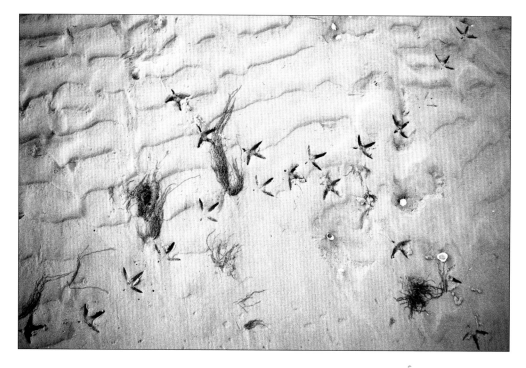

Footprints of a curlew (so I'm told!) in the muddy shoreline of Afon Braint – but is it of a single bird on an expedition, or two keeping a rendezvous?

Harvest for the bait diggers – again on the muddy foreshore of Afon Braint at Traeth Melynog.

Sunset on Traeth Melynog.

Ponies on Newborough Warren. The warren borders both Llanddwyn and Traeth Melynog and is part of an extensive nature reserve controlled by the Countryside Council for Wales. It is for environmental reasons that ponies have been selected for grazing purposes.

Bloody Cranesbill (*Geranium Sanguineum*). One of the many wild flowers found amongst the Newborough dunes.

The river Braint has its source on the slope of Mynydd Llwydiarth between Pentraeth and Llanddona on the eastern side of Anglesey, barely a mile from the shore of Red Wharf Bay. Being on the western side of the watershed however, it flows in the other direction, over twelve miles to the southwest, to join the Menai here at the edge of Traeth Melynog within sight of Caernarfon.

Thorny evidence of the prevailing winds.

A private dock at Plas Penrhyn on the Anglesey shore, with Caernarfon Castle centred over the entrance. In the nineteenth century Plas Penrhyn was owned by Humphrey Owen and then became the residence for his son, Captain William Humphrey Owen. Both father and son were leading Caernarfon businessmen and shipowners.

Tŷ Calch on the Arfon shore. Shown by that Welsh description on today's charts, it was shown by the English translation 'Limehouse' on Lewis Morris's chart of 1748.

Having left the *Mussel Bank* buoy to port, a mariner coming in from sea need only keep Tŷ Calch straight ahead to ensure a clear passage through the 'gap' into the Menai Strait itself.

The old Church at Llanfaglan on the mainland shore, looking northwesterly over the Menai Strait towards Newborough.

Caernarfon Castle skyline, front . . .

. . . and rear.

From Caernarfon to Port Dinorwic

The Castle's grandeur reflected in the still waters of Afon Seiont.

Segontium Terrace overlooking Cei Llechi (Slate Quay).

Segontium was the Romans' name for their outpost on the site which later became known as Caernarfon – while the quay was named after the thousands of tons of slates loaded there annually.

Known colloquially as *Bont'rabar* – formally Pont yr Aber – the Estuary Bridge swings open to allow passage for boats.

View from the swing bridge.

Despite its name, the *Floating Restaurant* will not in fact float until the tide has risen for a further two or three hours. Over the wall to the right can be seen the Courthouse while outside is the Anglesey Arms, a public house which provided a warm welcome for ferry passengers from Anglesey in days gone by, and remains a popular venue for many locals and visitors today.

The seaward face of the Anglesey Arms, and, on the right, the two barred windows of the cells in the old police station which adjoined the Courthouse.

Victoria Dock, Caernarfon

The dock was built in the 1870s to cater primarily for inward cargoes as the Slate Quay was fully committed to the outward slate traffic. The dock was the first part of what had been intended as a major port development, but the coming of the railway during the same period led to a reduction in sea transport and to curtailment of the grand design. Victoria Dock itself however was well utilised and remained active, discharging vessels until after World War II, when improving road transport finally made it redundant. Initially owned by the Caernarfon Harbour Trust, it was purchased by the County Council in order to create a haven for pleasure craft. In addition to those that have permanent berths at the pontoons, the dock is visited by some hundreds of cruising yachts each year.

A flap gate in the dock entrance opens about three hours before high water when the tide in the Strait has risen to the level of the water in the dock, and is closed again about half-ebb, to retain a minimum of two metres depth for the yachts in the dock to remain afloat.

'*Change*' – Yes, but of what exactly? Mind, clothes, money? Well, perhaps the best description would be a *keynote change*, for the following reason:

For the guidance of ships and boats approaching ports from seaward, buoys are laid to indicate the deep water channel with green conical buoys to the right (starboard) side and red can-shaped buoys to the left (port) side. When leaving port, of course, their aspect is reversed. Now in most rivers and waterways this arrangement is perfectly clear and logical, but the Menai Strait is not a normal waterway in this regard, as it has two 'front' entrances and has green conical buoys on the starboard side for vessels entering at both easterly and westerly ends. Clearly then, the sequence of buoyage from the two directions has to meet, and be reversed, at some point in the Strait and that agreed point is opposite Caernarfon - as indicated by the *change* buoy.

It could be expected that this buoy would be coloured both red and green but it is in fact of another type. While channel buoys are as already described, the other type are coloured black and yellow and called *cardinal* buoys; they indicate the extremities of individual hazards or dangers and are surmounted by two black cones differently arranged to show the side on which they should be passed. In the case of the *change* buoy, which happens to be sited to show the southern edge of a sandbank, the two cones pointing downward indicate that it should be passed on its southern side.

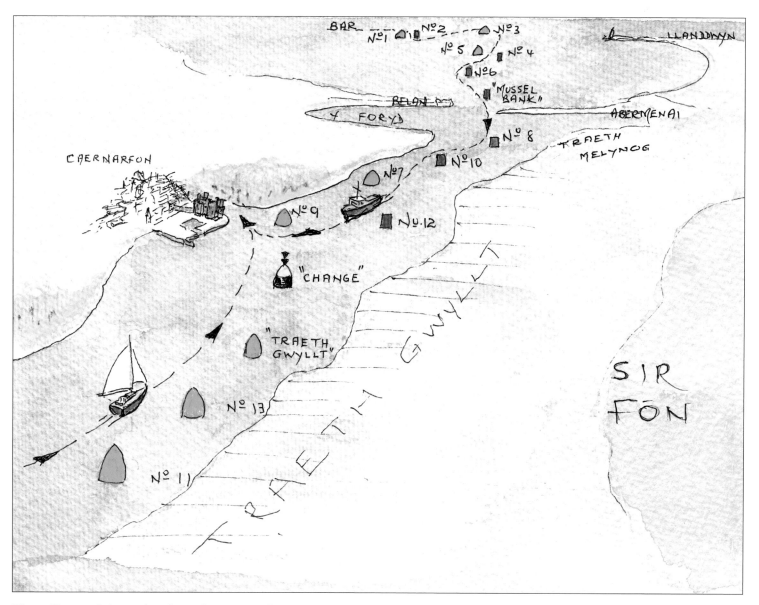

The sailing craft is coming from the Bangor direction and is keeping the green buoys to her starboard (right) side while making for Caernarfon – but so also is the motor launch coming in the opposite direction from seaward.

Should the sailing craft proceed past Caernarfon and out to sea then, after passing the *change* buoy, she will need to change the discipline and keep the green buoys to the port (left) side. Similarly, should the motor launch proceed past Caernarfon towards the east, then the green buoys previously kept to the starboard side will have to be kept to the port side after passing the *change* buoy.

Traeth Gwyllt – belying its name

Here again the word *traeth* means 'bank' rather than the more common 'beach', while *gwyllt* means 'wild' or 'unruly'. Known by this name for some centuries, its origin is uncertain as there are two logical possibilities: one is that it describes the bank's tendency to change its shape or form from one year to the next; the other is that it describes the boisterous conditions on and over the bank when the prevailing southwesterly winds are strong – particularly during strong ebb tides.

The latter is perhaps the more likely.

The old Tal-y-Foel ferry landing-stage on the Anglesey shore opposite Caernarfon.

The old landing again – with Caernarfon about a mile away.

This was the most important ferry at the western end of the Strait during the nineteenth century and the first half of the twentieth; the service came to an end in 1953, following the increase in private motor transport after World War II.

Before the introduction of public motor transport in the first part of the twentieth century, the passage by ferry to Caernarfon was far more convenient for the inhabitants of southwest Anglesey than the miles of narrow country roads to Llangefni or Menai Bridge. Considerable amounts of farm produce were carried for sale at Caernarfon market and in the opposite direction went foodstuffs and household goods purchased at the town's shops. As well as the farmers and their families, the general public who used the ferry included the schoolchildren who crossed on a daily basis to attend the then grammar school at Caernarfon.

Y Foel - Anglesey

Though the ferry originally ran from 'old' Tal y Foel about a mile to the westward, by the middle of the nineteenth century it had moved to this site (but retained its former title). From this time onwards it was the most important ferry at the western end of the Strait and was served by a steam vessel from 1849. Perhaps the dock visible in the background was the original landing but the increasing size of the ferry vessels and the limiting depths, particularly at low water, led to the need for the jetty seen in the two previous photographs.

The Sea Zoo.

A popular visitor attraction close to the shore of the Menai Strait at Brynsiencyn in Anglesey. In addition to displaying a great variety of fish and other marine wildlife, the establishment also breeds lobsters for restocking in local waters. It is here also that *Halen Môn* – Anglesey Salt – is processed after extraction from the salt water of the Menai. This product has achieved high regard in culinary circles in recent years.

Locally produced seafood – a tray of oysters from the beds worked by 'Menai Oysters' at their site on the shoreline below the Sea Zoo.

Trefarthen. A stately mansion on farm land facing the Strait.

Looking from Arfon to Anglesey over the waterside terrace of houses at Waterloo Port, a mile north of Caernarfon – with Traeth Gwyllt well exposed at low tide . . .

. . . and in the reverse direction, from Anglesey to Arfon and facing Waterloo Port.

(imagine the patience of the photographer waiting until there was one unmoving cormorant posing on each of the posts at the old Foel Jetty)

Ruins of the old Abbey at Plas Llanidan, Anglesey.

This delightful Menai-side cottage was developed from the old boathouse of Plas Llanidan. Until the closing years of the fifteenth century it was this site, or somewhere close by, that was the landing point for the ferry from Llanfairisgaer to Llanidan.

The old church of Llanfairisgaer in Arfon. In the Middle Ages both Llanidan and Llanfairisgaer were associated with the Priory at Beddgelert and there is a suggestion that the Prior (who had a house at Llanidan) may have been the holder of this ferry.

Plas Menai, a water-sports centre operated by the Sports Council for Wales and sited immediately adjacent to Llanfairisgaer church shown in the preceding photograph.

The Strait provides Plas Menai with ideal conditions for virtually all water-borne activities, having both shoal water and deep, banks, rocks and swift-flowing tides – all within reach of close supervision and safety facilities at the centre itself.

One of the centre's small craft in very quiet conditions (and displaying its 'home address').

Moel-y-Don, The Anglesey terminal of the ferry from Y Felinheli

It was here or hereabouts that the Romans crossed to Anglesey about 60 A.D. and it was here that a ferry (most probably moved from Llanidan) was established, under the Crown's authority, about 1500 A.D. Though operated by different tenants from time to time, it remained under the same authority until 1935 when it was transferred to the County Council. The service was maintained by them until 1958 when the falling demand led to its closure.

A particular category of passengers during the latter part of the nineteenth century, and the early part of the twentieth, were those Anglesey quarrymen who earned their livelihood at the Dinorwic Quarry, Llanberis. Early each Monday morning they crossed by the Moel-y-Don ferry and then travelled by narrow-gauge railway to the quarry where they lived in 'barracks' until the following Saturday when they returned to their Anglesey homes via the ferry.

Sad remains of a Thames sailing barge which ended its days far from home at Moel-y-Don. The owner had intended converting the craft to a houseboat – but the plan clearly failed!

Barley at harvest time and Llanedwen Church, Anglesey – two minutes' walk from the Menai shore – this is the Parish church which numbers the Marquis of Anglesey and family of Plas Newydd among its congregation. The barley reminds one of the old Welsh description of the island, which is displayed at the approach to the Menai Suspension Bridge, *Môn Mam Cymru* – literally 'Anglesey, Mother of Wales' but really meaning 'Granary of Wales'. This term reflects the reputation that the island (allegedly) produced sufficient foodstuff to sustain most of Wales during the Middle Ages.

Yachts wintering at Dinas boatyard at the southern extremity of Y Felinheli. The word *dinas* translates today as 'city' but in ancient times it usually meant a stronghold, established on high ground for both observation and defence. The wooded rise beyond the boats formed the original *dinas* and is on a promontory which provides a clear view of the Strait in both directions.

During the nineteenth century Dinas developed as a shipbuilding centre and in 1877 saw the launch of the largest wooden ship built in Gwynedd – the *Ordovic* of 877 gross tonnage.

Those who drive through Y Felinheli may gain the impression that the village is a narrow ribbon development following the pattern in industrial areas – but from off-shore it can be seen that it has both width and height as well as length.

Looking northeast, Y Felinheli Sailing Club in the foreground and Moel-y-Don to the left, on the Anglesey shore.

A wintry view of the foreshore at Y Felinheli. The slipway in the foreground was the landing for the ferry mentioned on page 37.

Just right of centre in the photograph can be seen the outer gates of the lock giving access to Port Dinorwic dock. The tide is low and it will be two or three hours before there is sufficient water for the gates to be opened.

Y Felinheli was the original name of the village but, with the development of the port to load the slate produce from the Dinorwig quarries at Llanberis, the name Port Dinorwic was adopted in shipping and business circles. By today however, the original name has been formally, and firmly, re-established as the proper postal address, although 'Port Dinorwic' remains the normal description for the dock as a maritime facility and destination.

PORT DINORWIC TO MENAI BRIDGE

Inside the dock, Port Dinorwic. Winter sun on boats awaiting summer.

Water overflowing from the dock into the Menai Strait. Passage through these lock gates was the start of some thousands of voyages for ships carrying Dinorwig slates to distant ports. During the peak years at the end of the nineteenth century and beginning of the twentieth, over 70,000 tons were exported annually.

Looking back along the Menai to the southwest from Faenol park on the Arfon shore. Moel-y-Don (opposite Port Dinorwic) is in the centre and the tip of Traeth Gwyllt just showing on the extreme right, while to the left are the unmistakable peaks of the the Rivals (Yr Eifl).

Boathouse and dock on the Faenol shore opposite Plas Newydd, dry at low water on a spring tide. Early ordnance survey maps record the name of the site as *Tŷ Glo* – literally 'Coal House' which suggests that this was the landing point (and storage) for small sailing vessels delivering coal to the Faenol estate. The coming of the railway in the 1860s would have provided a more convenient and economical delivery service, and the end of seaborne coal to Tŷ Glo.

A private dock at Plas Newydd on the Anglesey shore, not a commercial facility but one primarily created to serve the family's pleasure craft. From the middle of the twentieth century, and starting with H.M.S. *Conway* which was moored nearby in 1949, it has been used by a succession of training and educational bodies as a centre for instruction in marine skills and watersports. Y Felinheli can be seen on the opposite shore on the extreme right.

Whatever one might feel about the privileges of the landed gentry in days gone by, one can only admire the handsome buildings and glorious gardens created by them – initially for their own benefit but indirectly for the good of the neighbourhood as well.

Plas Newydd, the family home of the Pagets, shown here with Britannia Bridge in the background is a delightful example. Though now in the ownership of the National Trust, it remains the home of the present Marquis of Anglesey.

Pwll Fanogl – Anglesey

The cottage on the left is the home of the renowned artist Sir Kyffin Williams, and the building on the right was at one time both a warehouse and factory. At the beginning of the twentieth century, the creek was full of activity with ships discharging household supplies, coal and other goods for the local population and loading local produce such as salt pork and, quite surprisingly, margarine manufactured on the site. Another factory at Pwllfanogl produced school slates which were also shipped in considerable quantities.

There is very deep water in this particular part of the Menai and in 1976, in a position close to that from which this photograph was taken, divers from Bangor University's Department of Oceanography discovered a large quantity of dressed slates on the sea-bed. The form of the 'stack' suggested that it was the cargo of a ship that had sunk at the site even though no remains of the vessel had survived. Both size and shape of the slates are unique and it is thought that they date from the sixteenth century.

This memorial to Nelson stands at an out-of-the-way spot on the shore below Plas Llanfair on the Anglesey shore. It was created by Admiral Lord Clarence Paget who lived in the mansion and who was an enthusiastic amateur sculptor.

Facing away from the land, the statue was clearly not intended for the convenience of public gaze, but it was really beyond the close appraisal of mariners as well, as most waterborne traffic follows the main channel on the opposite, mainland, shore. In later years however it did serve a useful purpose. A navigational mark was built on high ground further to the east on the railway embankment and an imaginary line from that mark and over Nelson's statue served as a leading line to guide ships clear of an underwater hazard known as Carreg Ginnog close to the Faenol shore.

Doubtless including the Scots, Irish and Welsh crew members!

Rear view of the statue in a morning mist – with the sea as still as the stone.

Eglwys y Santes Fair – The Church of Saint Mary, the second of that name on the same site, and the source of the name Plas Llanfair on the nearby mansion. The Welsh *plas,* though doubtless of the same origin as the French 'palais' and English 'palace', translates in practical terms as 'Hall'; for example, the Plas Llanfair mentioned here might in England have been termed 'St. Mary's Hall' or perhaps 'Marychurch Hall'.

Having been the home of Admiral Lord Clarence Paget at one time, the nautical connection was renewed from the 1940s when it became home to the training establishment *Indefatigable*. St. Mary's was the parish church for the family in their day and then for the sea school until that establishment closed in 1995.

This striking stained-glass window was installed in recognition of the officers and boys of the *Indefatigable* who attended services in St. Mary's for half a century.

49

A striking view of Britannia bridge from the shore below St. Mary's Church at the start of a summer's day – but how did the bridge acquire its name? In mid-stream there is a rock shown on the chart (page 53) as 'Britannia Rock' which carries the centre column of the bridge and it might be supposed that the bridge took its name naturally from that rock. In the middle of Queen Victoria's reign it would have been difficult to find anything more appropriate, but that is not the full story.

As shown on various maps of the area, the original Welsh name for the rock was Carreg Frydan, which is thought to describe the behaviour of the tidal stream flowing about the rock; a rough English translation might be 'turbulence rock'. It is a possibility that misinterpretation of the spoken description *Frydan* led to its being recorded as *Frydain,* and for that word to have been assumed to convey the adjectival form of the word *Prydain*, the Welsh for 'Britain'. Well, the derivation of place names is fraught with difficulties, but the Welsh name of the rock is still Carreg Frydan, although the bridge has long since been known as Pont Britannia.

Built by Robert Stephenson in 1850 to carry the then new railway, it was rebuilt to carry both rail and road in 1970 following a disastrous fire, which seriously damaged the original tube sections. To mariners the bridge is taken to be the western limit of that turbulent part of the Strait known as the 'Swellies' (Pwll Ceris in Welsh), which extends for a mile from here to the eastern limit at the Suspension Bridge. *Ceris* in the Welsh name is thought to date from the sixth century when there was a local leader of that name; while the English term 'Swelly' is thought to derive from the word 'swallow' which was said to be the fate of unfortunate ships caught in the fierce swirling tide, and certainly conveys a proper sense of awe!

Can you see the reflection of the old bridge in the waters of the Strait ? The photographer advises that it can be seen by any careful observer after closing-time on nights of full moon!

A section of the original tube which carried the rail track and which has been kept for historical purposes. Unfortunately, although close to the bridge, it is not visible from the public thoroughfares but the site can be visited by following the path down toward the Strait from Treborth on the southern side of the bridge.

One of the pair of stone lions guarding the approaches to the Britannia Bridge rail-crossings. A nonsense rhyme describing them in Welsh at the time of building can be translated as:

Two bald lions, both quite fat,
Two on this side, two on that.

51

THE SWELLIES (Pwll Ceris)

Before proceeding further eastwards, it may be useful to consider some of the Swellies' characteristics, while referring to the section of Admiralty chart 1464 'Menai Strait', reproduced on page 53 opposite. During the passage so far the greatest danger to ships and boats has been the shoal water over the sandbanks and shores, but after passing Britannia Bridge the picture changes completely. The main channel through the Swellies is narrow, having the rock-bound mainland shore on the one side, and the Cribbin and Swelly Rocks on the other.

In addition to the rocky islands and reefs that are obvious hazards to vessels of all sizes, the nature and rate of the tidal flow, together occasionally with the wind effect, can cause considerable difficulty for the unwary. At certain times of tide there may be as much as a metre of difference in the sea level at the two ends of the Swellies and this, combined with the restricted width causes rates of flow of up to eight knots at spring tides and up to five knots even at neaps. Great care is clearly required and unless a craft has a powerful engine the passage should only be made at slack water when the tidal flow slows prior to changing direction. At neap tides the slack water period lasts for perhaps forty minutes but at spring tides it lasts for barely twenty minutes.

An old English translation from a Latin manuscript reads as follows:

In that arm of the sea that departeth between this island Mon and North Wales is a swelowe that draweth to schippes that seileth and sweloweth them in as doth Scylla and Charybdis – therefore we may nouzt seile by this swalowe but slily at the full see. In other words, one should only venture through the Swellies at high-water slack, and with care.

It is possible for small craft to make the passage at low-water slack, but the channel depth and width is even further restricted at such times.

Despite the potential dangers however, the Swellies has many attractive characteristics including Ynys Gored Goch. For many centuries the island, with its weir fishery rights, was held by the Bangor Diocese, and one early Bishop was known as Madog Goch (Red Madog). The island therefore became known as Ynys Gored Madog Goch – 'the island of Red Madog's weir', but with the passage of time this was abbreviated to the present Ynys Gored Goch. The island was sold by the Diocese in 1888 but the weir fishery remained in operation for a further half century.

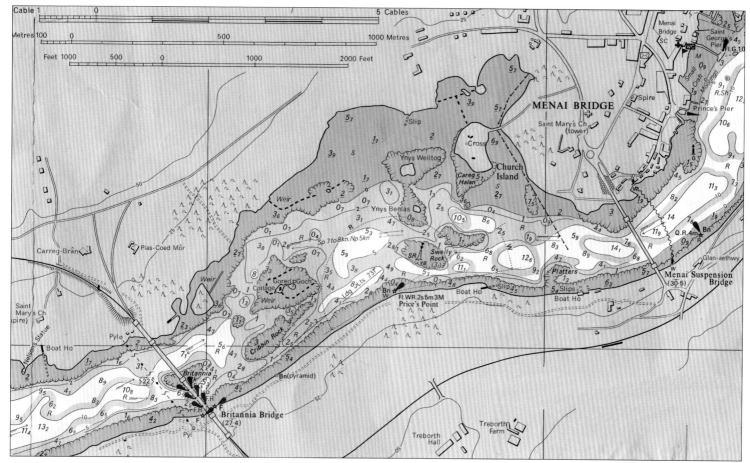

Part of *Admiralty Chart* 1464, 'Menai Strait' (Chart 4).

A WORD ABOUT THE TIDES

One cannot really follow the flow of the Menai, nor the movement of the ships and boats that traverse it, without some appreciation of the tides. The following offers a basic explanation.

The attraction of the moon is the most influential factor causing tidal movements, and it is these lunar movements which lead to the time of high water being later each day and for its height to vary. On the days of full and new moon, which occurs every fortnight, the tide rises to its highest level and falls to its lowest – the so-called 'spring' tides. While this is the theoretical case, natural time-lag usually results in the highest tides actually occurring two or three days after full and new moon. With the moon at its quarter and three-quarters however, its effect is least and the tides do not rise, or fall, as far and these smaller tides are known as 'neaps'. At spring tides, the waters not only rise higher but flow faster (as there is a greater volume moving in the same period of time). This is an important factor for mariners working in restricted waters such as the Menai.

At each site on the coastline, the time of high water on days of full and new moon is constant. For example, at Llanddwyn it occurs at about a quarter-past nine, while at Penmon it is at half-past ten (these are on local time not G.M.T). Every day thereafter the time of high water is about fifty minutes later until the completion of the lunar cycle at the next full or new moon.

The tides on the coast of Wales follow the general pattern in the Irish Sea, the flood stream flowing in a northerly direction for six hours before reversing and flowing to the southward during six hours of ebb. Some of the huge northerly flow on the flood diverts to fill Caernarfon Bay and then enters the Strait past Llanddwyn; it continues to the eastward past Caernarfon, through the Swellies and past Bangor until it meets the other part of the flood stream entering the Strait from the other direction in the vicinity of Penmon. This later component of the flood has streamed past the outer coastline of Anglesey and of course, having travelled that much further, it understandably arrives at Penmon an hour or more after the first part arrived at Llanddwyn. This is why high water at Beaumaris is an hour later than at Caernarfon.

Once the east-going flood stream does meet its 'other half' a little to the northwest of Penmon, it promptly reverses direction and flows back to the westward, although its height is continuing to rise for a considerable time at Beaumaris and Bangor. The place most affected by this peculiarity is the Swellies, where the sea level continues to rise for an hour and a half or so after slack water when the stream changes direction.

It is clear then that the direction and height of tide, coupled with the times of high and low water, result in the tides having a material bearing on the movement of every boat (and fish!) in the Menai Strait, and so adding to its interest and intrigue.

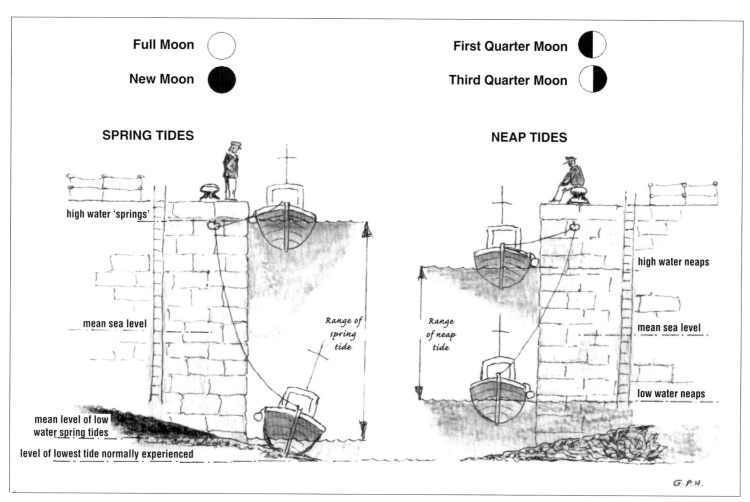

Full Moon ○

New Moon ●

First Quarter Moon ◗

Third Quarter Moon ◖

SPRING TIDES

high water 'springs'

mean sea level

Range of spring tide

mean level of low water spring tides

level of lowest tide normally experienced

NEAP TIDES

high water neaps

mean sea level

low water neaps

Range of neap tide

G.P.H.

The variation of the tides – each lunar month.

Britannia Rock, Carreg Frydan (top right), the foundation for the bridge's centre column, with the northern arch reflected in the quiet water at low-water slack.

Looking down on Britannia Rock with Ynys Gored Goch (top left) and the Cribbin Rock (top right).

By night the red, white and green lights below the southern arch of the bridge provide a clear indication of its general position. In order to keep in the narrow approach channel however, the mariner must keep the two leading lights (below the landward end of the arch) in line, one above the other. This photograph was taken from the Anglesey foreshore, looking westward, which explains why the Swelly Rock light appears on the left.

Where Anglesey once exported grain, it now sends power to the National Grid from the Wylfa nuclear power station, crossing the Menai Strait here just south of the Britannia Bridge.

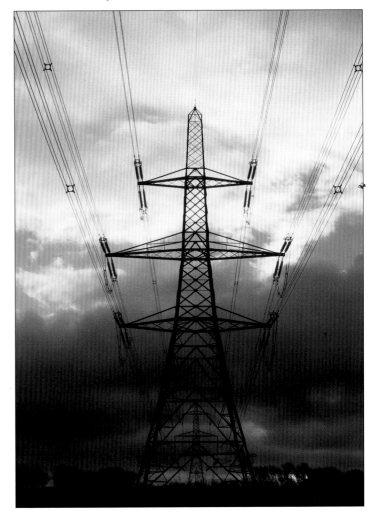

Shadow of the southern arch over the main channel with two tips of the Cribbin rock just showing above water between Ynys Gored Goch and the mainland, probably about three hours before high water. At this point, the main channel lies between Cribbin rock and the wooded, but rocky, mainland shore (refer to chart 4 on page 53).

The dangerous nature of the Cribbin rock displayed at low water of a spring tide, with a glimpse of the Suspension Bridge in the distance.

The name of the rock is from the Welsh *crib* - a comb, and *cribin* – a rake. In this particular context it might in English have been christened 'the coxcomb' as it is really a reef or ridge of rock.

Slack water high, with two boats passing before Ynys Gored Goch – a sylvan scene with the Cribbin rock hidden from sight!

Spring ebb flowing strongly over the fish weir on the northern side of the island.

Swelly Rock beacon at high water on a spring tide – but, as explained on page 54, the ebb stream has been running fiercely for over an hour by this time.

The same beacon six hours later at low water. The sea level here rises by about eighteen feet on spring tides. The two inverted cones indicate (as was the case at the *change* buoy) that the beacon is at the southern extremity of the danger and that craft should therefore pass on its southern side.

Thrift (*Armeria Maritima*) shows among the rock along the Anglesey shore of the Swellies and on its numerous islets.

The Church of St.Tysilio in summer . . .

A place of worship was first established on what is now called 'Church Island' by St. Tysilio in the sixth century. By about the fifteenth century, the building had been extended to its present form and at some time an embankment had been built to provide access to/from the Anglesey shore at any stage of the tide.

Though close to the hazardous waters of the Swellies, the narrowness of the Strait in the vicinity of Menai Bridge makes it a convenient site for a ferry, as shown by the written records from the twelfth century onwards. It is probable of course that the site was a crossing place long before written records, and could have been the one used by St. Tysilio when he first arrived in the area.

It may well have been the practice for some ferry passengers to visit the Church to seek a blessing for their safety before embarking, and for others to visit in order to give thanks for their safe deliverance.

. . . and in winter.

The rocks seen here just west of the Suspension Bridge off the mainland shore are known as the 'Platters' and can only be seen at low water on a spring tide. They are a significant hazard to vessels passing through the Swellies, as they lie close to the line of the main channel between the Swelly rock and the centre of the bridge. Many craft have been lost or damaged over the years by striking them.

Undoubtedly however, the most spectacular loss was that of the training ship H.M.S. *Conway* in April 1953. Launched as the 92-gun wooden battleship H.M.S. Nile in 1833, the ship had served as a school ship on the Mersey from 1872 until 1941 when she was moved to the Strait during the *Blitz*.

First moored off Bangor pier, the ship was moved to a mooring off Plas Newydd in 1949 and in 1953 was being moved back to Bangor before being towed to Birkenhead for dry-docking later in the year. The largest vessel ever to make the Swellies passage, the *Conway* needed a high spring tide to ensure sufficient depth of water but, as explained earlier, such tides have the shortest period of slack water and the fastest flowing tides. The operation was however just possible – providing nothing went wrong. In the event, a combination of circumstances resulted in the ship failing to reach the Suspension Bridge before the adverse tidal stream commenced and its increasing strength led to the tugs losing control and the ship being forced ashore inside the Platters.

Hen Felin (old mill)

A waterside cottage on the mainland shore immediately south of the bridge. It is difficult to imagine a working mill on such a site but perhaps it was a loading point for produce from Treborth Mill at some time in the past.

Seaweed and sunshine in the tidal 'front garden'.

Menai Suspension Bridge . . . to the Welsh, Pont y Borth

Here we have the word *porth* again but with the *p* softened to *b* by mutation. In this case *porth* refers to Porthaethwy, the haven, (landing or port) of Aethwy who was a local leader many centuries ago and who gave his name to Tindaethwy, the commote which embraced much of southeast Anglesey.

Porthaethwy, (usually abbreviated to *Y Borth*) had been the name of the adjacent settlement since time immemorial. To the politicians, surveyors, engineers and administrators however, the locality became the site where a bridge was being built over the Menai and they might well have spoken of the 'Menai Strait Bridge' and in turn to ' The Menai Bridge' and then just 'Menai Bridge'. Doubtless it was an easier description than Porthaethwy, and indeed it became common parlance to many Welsh people as well as English, although the majority of the Welsh today still use the original name.

The magnificent feat of engineering embodied in the building of the bridge by Telford in 1826 saw an immediate end to the local ferry which had been all-important for centuries, but brought huge improvements in the Anglesey/Mainland transport and communications.

Extolled by innumerable poets and writers and a regular subject for photographers, this particular winter view of the bridge was taken from the steep wooded foreshore below Treborth Hall.

FROM MENAI BRIDGE TO ABEROGWEN

The same bridge, and in the winter again, but given an entirely different impression by the floodlights – not quite San Francisco, but an impressive 'Golden Gate' nonetheless.

An unusual view of Menai Bridge with a January sun casting long shadows of the bridge over the houses.

Timber yard and wharf, Menai Bridge

Davies's y Borth – (the Davies's of Menai Bridge) was the name of a substantial local sailing-ship company which traded world-wide during the second half of the nineteenth century.

Originally merchants in Llangefni who first ventured into shipping to carry their own goods, they purchased the wharf and warehouse at Menai Bridge in 1828. In the following years they bought larger vessels which were employed carrying slate and emigrants from the Strait to North America, and returning with timber from such places as Quebec and St. John's Newfoundland.

At that time there was considerable local demand for timber, by house builders, quarry operators, and shipbuilders – but with no material source in Anglesey or the adjacent mainland, it was more economical to bring whole shiploads direct to the Strait from North America, rather than bring it in individual cartloads along narrow mountainous tracks from the wooded areas of North Wales.

During its final period the company operated large sailing ships on a world-wide basis but while they no longer traded to Menai Bridge, they kept their controlling headquarters there until they discontinued business at the beginning of the twentieth century.

Ships from Scandinavia continued to discharge timber to the wharf in the photograph until after World War II, but today the supplies are delivered by road from the major ports.

The 'Liverpool Arms' public house close to the waterfront at Menai Bridge.

It was no wonder that Liverpool was known as the capital of Wales (well North Wales anyway!) for well over a hundred years, from the early nineteenth century to the middle of the twentieth, as that was the most conveniently reached metropolis, and for more than half that period, sea transport was the prime route for both goods and people. There were regular steamship services from the Mersey to the Strait, with two or three calls each week at Beaumaris, Bangor, Menai Bridge, and arrangements for Caernarfon as well. Incidentally, Beaumaris also has its 'Liverpool Arms'.

Ships no longer call at Menai Bridge to land goods or passengers, apart from an occasional visit by such as the excursion vessel *Balmoral* – but still, a new pier was built to take the place of the original 'St. George's Pier' when that structure was demolished.

In addition to its occasional use for passengers and yachts, the pier's prime purpose is to provide a semi-permanent berth for the *Prince Madog*, the research vessel attached to Bangor University's Department of Ocean Sciences which is based at Menai Bridge.

Lying at the end of the pier in this night-time view, can be seen the original *Prince Madog* whose working life came to an end in 2001 when she was replaced by a more modern vessel.

The pier in daylight with the new *Prince Madog* alongside.

Only two British universities have a Department of Ocean Sciences, and of the two, only Bangor has a specially-designed research vessel. From its extensive site at Menai Bridge, the Department has developed an acclaimed international reputation and brought great credit to the University.

The photograph shows the Department's quayside laboratories, within convenient reach of the *Prince Madog*'s pier berth.

The 'old' *Prince Madog* off the Anglesey shore approaching Menai Bridge.

Madog was a son of Owain Gwynedd, who ruled North Wales from 1137 to 1170. It was Madog who (allegedly!) discovered America in the twelfth century, some three hundred years before Columbus. Mythical or not, the story of Madog has inspired poets, songwriters and historians to compose and research for many centuries and no better name could be found for the University's research vessel!

The new vessel in 2001 – with the Carneddau mountain range rising in the background.

The 'new' bridge over the River Cadnant reflected in the Menai on a cold and calm winter's morning.

At the eastern fringe of Menai Bridge, the Cadnant estuary was the landing point of another ferry over the Strait. This one was known as the Bishop's Ferry.

Looking out from the Cadnant to Ynys Castell – 'Castle Island'.

Looking westward towards Menai Bridge – the crossing route for the Bishop's ferry was from the Cadnant estuary beyond the island on the right, to the creek on the left known as Porth yr Esgob (Bishop's Haven) on the Bangor shore.

Porth yr Esgob and the house now known as 'Water's Edge'. Extending from the shore in this area can be seen the remains of a fish weir known as Gored y Git (or Gút for the derivation is uncertain) – the name now used for the site itself and for the road leading to it from Siliwen, Bangor.

Old cottages on the western shore of the Cadnant estuary. It is probable that this was the landing site for the Bishop's Ferry when the tide so allowed. The old Cadnant bridge is in the background.

A genuine 'riverside residence' – on the eastern shore of the Cadnant upstream of the old bridge.

Part of Glyn Garth showing Plas Rhianfa.

This section of the Menai shore between the Cadnant and the Gazelle Hotel saw the building of many palatial properties during the second half of the nineteenth century, a number by Liverpool-based business and shipping families. While many of the properties appear of relatively modest proportions when viewed from the Menai Bridge to Beaumaris road, their appearance from seaward is far more imposing, with the buildings and land extending down to the edge of the Strait.

University boat crews practise in ideal rowing conditions – calm.

An August regatta with the sailing boats in *their* ideal conditions – a spanking breeze.

Bangor Pier in all its glory shortly before sunset. It was built in 1896 when there was considerable competition between seaside towns to attract holidaymakers, and whilst Llandudno and Rhyl had the best beaches, Bangor made sure that it had the longest pier!

A quarter of a mile in length, it extends precisely half-way across the Strait, almost to the red buoy seen just to the left of the pierhead. That buoy marks the southern limit of the deep water channel which follows the Anglesey shore at this point. The length of the pier allowed passenger vessels and ferry craft to berth at its end in almost all tidal conditions.

With a warm welcome in the adjacent hostelry, and a convenient slipway, this site is today extremely popular with fair-weather sailors – but until the middle of the twentieth century it was the Anglesey landing for the Garth ferry from Bangor.

It was known as Borthwen in the sixteenth century and for many years the ferryman's house was known as Borthwen Bach. However, since the building of a hotel (named the *Gazelle*) on the site in the nineteenth century, the place and the slipway have become known by the same name.

Immediately east of the pier at the Garth, this slipway was the high-water landing for the ferry on the Bangor side of the Strait. At low water, before the days of the pier, ferry passengers had to struggle over the muddy foreshore to reach the boat at the edge of the channel, but once the pier was built, the ferry could berth at its seaward end where passengers could embark and disembark without difficulty.

The earliest ferries were propelled by oars but there are accounts of sailing craft as well at the end of the nineteenth century. In 1917 the Bangor Council bought a steam passenger vessel named *Cynfal* to serve as a ferry and also as an occasional tender to the excursion steamers. Perhaps she was too expensive to maintain but for whatever reason she was replaced by a motor launch from 1929 until the service finally ceased in the 1970s.

The *Gazelle* again but at high water this time and with a good crowd watching the sailing. The red buoy with the name *Bangor* is the one noted in the photograph on page 76.

The spectacular view from Llandegfan about 250 feet (75m) above sea level.

From this position it is difficult to appreciate that the pier only extends half way across the Strait from the Garth to the *Gazelle*. In the middle distance to the left is Port Penrhyn while the inshore area to the right is known as Hirael Bay.

Wintering yachts at Dickies boatyard at the Garth, Bangor. A considerable number of commercial sailing vessels were built in the area during the nineteenth century and the tradition was continued during the first half of the twentieth century although by then most of the craft being built were pleasure yachts. Notable exceptions were the naval craft constructed during World War II which included motor torpedo-boats, motor gun-boats and rescue launches.

No longer involved with the building of boats, Dickies remains a very active boatyard with sale, storage and repair facilities, used, amongst many others, by the RNLI, one of whose lifeboats is seen here.

A mussel dredger heading for the entrance to Port Penrhyn. The two headlands in the background are Penmaen Mawr and Penmaen Bach. *Pen* means head, or top, *maen* means stone, but in this particular context might be translated as 'crag', while *mawr* and *bach* mean large and small respectively.

The dock is in fact an open basin and after a few hours' ebb its bed is dry – well, muddy at least, but at high water there is plenty of depth for such craft as the mussel dredger, seen here, to berth at the quayside and discharge. The letters ' BS ' signify that she is registered at Beaumaris and numbered 449.

About the middle of the nineteenth century, much of the slate produced by the Penrhyn quarry was exported to North America and during the second half of that century the slate exported (to all destinations) amounted to more than 100,000 tons annually.

In the twentieth century however, there came both a reduction in demand and an increase in the tonnage handled by rail. In consequence, the amount of slate shipped from Port Penrhyn steadily reduced and finally ceased entirely, leaving the dock largely disused. In recent years however the facility has seen renewed activity with occasional calls by commercial vessels and regular use by the mussel fishery. The quayside areas also house a number of marine associated businesses, including one specialising in the restoration of wooden boats.

Here is a fine example of that particular shipwright's skill.

The river Cegin and the outer quay wall of Port Penrhyn at low water.

Until about 1770, most of the slates produced in the district were loaded into ships at Aberogwen, a mile or so to the east and the other side of the promontory on which Penrhyn Castle stands; thereafter Abercegin became the preferred site and in 1790 a proper quay was built there when it became known as Port Penrhyn. Originally about 500 feet in length, the quay was extended over the years and eventually incorporated in the development of the dock as we see it today.

1801 saw the opening of a horse-drawn railway from the port to Penrhyn Quarry over six miles distant, a pioneering enterprise which materially reduced the costs of transporting the slate to the point of shipment.

An elegantly-designed and well-ventilated roundhouse on Port Penrhyn quay – actually a convenience for the waterfront workers!

Another of the mussel dredgers lying alongside, this is the vessel seen dredging for seed-mussels in the photograph on page 6. The letters 'LR' on her side signify that her registry is at Lerwick in the Shetlands.

These are the heavy dredge nets used to harvest the mussels on the Lavan sands and the adjacent Bangor Flats. The local inhabitants have collected various shellfish from these grounds for generations but it is only in recent years that the fishery has been properly developed on a commercial basis. The annual harvest landed at Port Penrhyn varies between three and ten thousand tons, the vast majority being exported to France.

This is an example of a mussel bed at low water. Each company or operating vessel (four in 2002) that works the beds is allocated a specific area of the sea bed and their first task is to obtain the seed-mussels to 'sow' there. Most of these are dredged in the western approaches to the Strait when they are about half an inch (12mm) in length.

For a variety of reasons the waters there (amongst other sites in the Irish Sea) are well-suited to the mussels' early breeding growth, but it is the waters at the eastern end that provide the best conditions for their development thereafter – hence the 'transplanting' procedure. They are then left to grow to about one inch (25mm.) before being harvested for market. As seen in the lower photograph, a fully grown mussel is much larger again but by then the shell has attracted a supernumary growth of a variety of smaller shells which make it less appealing to buyers.

Penrhyn Castle from the eastward.

The present building, on the site of the former mansion was built in the pseudo-Norman style by Thomas Hopper in 1827. Solid and imposing it reflects the position and authority of the Pennant family – and the wealth stemming from their plantation property in Jamaica and then their most lucrative quarry undertaking at Bethesda.

Penrhyn means 'promontory', and the castle does literally stand on the promontory between the estuary of the Cegin to the westward and that of the Ogwen to the eastward.

Cast-iron bridge over the river Ogwen where it reaches the shore of the Menai.

The following words can be seen in the bridge casting:

CAST AT PENYDARRAN IRONWORKS, GLAMORGANSHIRE. MDCCCXXIV

As mentioned earlier, it was at Aberogwen that ships loaded the local slate produce from the fourteenth century until late in the 1790s when, about thirty years before the building of this bridge in 1824, the shipping process was transferred to Abercegin.

From this point, following the ebb, the Ogwen creates a channel which forms the western limit of the Lavan Sands, and at low water it meets the main stream of the Menai close to the Anglesey shore, a little west of Gallows Point (see map 8). The best view of the bridge calls for wet feet, or better still a boat!

The ironworks at Merthyr Tydfil in South Wales were established towards the end of the eighteenth century, a little before the opening of the Glamorganshire Canal. This waterway was of great advantage to the new industry as it allowed for the transport of its produce to Cardiff for onward shipment to any port in the kingdom.

Though built in a number of parts, each section of the bridge would weigh some tons and their discharge from the coasting vessel and erection on site must have been quite a feat for both sailors and builders.

Within a short distance of the bridge there is a nature reserve visited by birdwatchers who come to observe shore and estuary birds in particular. The reeds seen in the photograph (*Phragmites Communis*), which lie adjacent to the Ogwen above the bridge, provide nesting for a variety of species.

Remnants of sea defences just eastward of the Ogwen estuary. (The bolt holes suggest that the timbers may have had an earlier life as railway sleepers.) The edge of the land along this shore is subject to erosion by the tidal waters of the Menai.

The swans are some of the sixty or so which frequent the estuary during the summer.

For centuries before the making of good roads to Bangor and the ferry at Porthaethwy, travellers on their way to Anglesey from the eastward crossed the Lavan Sands by foot or horseback to reach the Beaumaris ferry boat at the edge of the sands opposite that town. Commencing the four-mile journey from the mainland as soon as the sands 'dried' about three hours after high water, they could only hope that the boat would be waiting for them, or would respond to their calls, when they arrived at the water's edge. Though relatively narrow by low water, the Menai was still a serious hazard because of its depth and rate of flow.

In earlier times, most travellers followed the tracks over the sands from the vicinity of Penmaenmawr but during the eighteenth century, Abergwyngregyn became the most common starting point; by that time also, the Anglesey ferry point had been moved from a position opposite the town to one opposite Gallows Point.

Improvement in the roads towards Bangor led to an increase in the number of travellers who preferred the safer crossing at Porthaethwy, and a corresponding decrease in the numbers using the Lavan Sands route. Finally, with the opening of the Suspension Bridge in 1826, the Beaumaris ferry became redundant and it was officially discontinued in February 1830.

About three hours before high water, the sea once again hides the sands completely. So, unique amongst the ferries over the Strait, the Beaumaris ferry only worked during the five or six hours between half-ebb and half-flood and, in all probability, did not operate during the hours of darkness.

Lavan Sands at low water. Gallows Point can be seen at the extreme left and Beaumaris town on the right.

Lavan Sands Crossing

About 1460, in a poetical composition called a *cywydd*, a poet known as Rhys Goch of Glandyfrdwy included the following couplet referring to the Lavan Sands crossing:

> *I dir Môn er dŵr Menai,*
> *Dros y traeth ond aros trai*

This can be translated as follows:

> To Mona's shores 'spite Menai's flow
> The sands are crossed when tide is low

The view from Anglesey towards Penrhyn Castle with the tip of Gallows Point, where the ferry landed, showing on the right. On the left is the opposing tip of the Lavan Sands which extend from the mainland; at low water on a spring tide the distance between the two points is as little as two hundred yards.

Looking to the eastward from Gallows Point with Penmaenmawr on the right. The distance over the sands on this route was (and is!) four miles or more. Those that were late embarking on their journey over the sands had to be sure that they had sufficient time to reach the far shore before they were caught by the next incoming tide.

View over Gallows Point towards Aberogwen and the Carneddau.

The Point again on a winter's afternoon. Being the site of the North West Venturers Sailing Club, the area is full of activitiy during the summer but the only boats visible here are safely ashore in their winter berths.

At one time there was a public refuse tip sited at the Point and that was probably the source of these glass fragments found on the foreshore.

Beaumaris from Lavan Sands, early on a Spring morning (left) and from the edge of the sands (below).

Although the channel of the Menai here is obviously narrow, it is nevertheless deep – about eight metres even at low-water spring tides.

The western end of the town.

Until recent times marine Admiralty charts showed depths in fathoms but with the all-pervading desire to adopt European standards, metric units have been adopted and the word 'fathom' which has served us so long is fast being forgotten. The Welsh word is *gwryd* – or more correctly *gwrhyd* – *gwr* and *hyd*, literally 'man' and 'length'. It is likely however that this word, like 'fathom', will also fall victim to the metric tide and both languages will have lost traditional words that have served us well.

A calm autumn morning looking over Beaumaris town with the Great Orme's Head (Y Gogarth) beyond.

Beaumaris pier – built originally to serve the steamers that carried both passengers and cargo between Liverpool and the Strait. Those commercial days have long since gone but the pier remains an attraction for promenaders and provides a good facility for excursion craft and fishermen.

Winter sunrise through the pier's structure.

The lower beams are home to the Plumose Anemone (*Metridium Senile*) – whose appearance improves when submerged!

Part of the entrance and moat, Beaumaris Castle. It has been suggested that there was a connection between the Moat and the Menai which allowed supply craft to berth under the castle wall and discharge goods direct through the low opening seen on the right. If this was the case then its use would probably have been restricted to periods of high spring tides.

Though the photograph shows the Strait appearing as a broad waterway beyond the Castle, most of the width between the shores is occupied by the Lavan Sands covered by a few feet of water at high tide, while the navigable channel is in fact only five hundred yards from the castle walls.

Dinghies and other small craft being prepared for the regatta at the edge of the 'Green'.

It was to and from this vicinity that the ferry to the edge of the sands operated for many centuries. Earliest records refer to it as the Llanfaes ferry as that was the name of the nearest settlement but, after the building of the new town and Castle by Edward I, it became known as the Beaumaris ferry although it operated from the same site. It remained there until about the beginning of the eighteenth century when it was moved westward to Gallows Point for operational reasons.

East of Beaumaris the nature of the foreshore changes completely and the adjacent agricultural land is composed of clays from the ice-age containing gravel and sand left by the melting ice. The photograph shows the open face of the eroded land, with the finer constituents washed away and the larger rocks and stones left exposed.

From here, at the easternmost point of Anglesey – from Penmon quarry on the southern side, to the Dinmor quarry half a mile away on the northern side, thousands of tons of limestone were quarried for many building projects over the years . Used extensively in Edward 1's castles, and again by Stephenson and Telford in their bridges, the material was also quarried during the nineteenth century for the construction of the docks in Liverpool and also for major public buildings and large offices in that city. During the twentieth century a prodigious amount of the stone was shipped by hopper vessels to the Mersey estuary where it was discharged to form the training banks known as *revetments*. These were built up on either side of the main channel from the sea to the river entrance in order to control its direction and depth.

As that task came to an end there came a further requirement for stone for the construction of the then new Seaforth Dock until that project was completed in the 1970s. Since that time, no further demand has arisen so the quarries have been closed and the jetties demolished, but very recently, in the new millennium, some of the old quarry workings have been developed as fish farms.

Penmon Quarry.

Penmon Priory, with the dovecote on the right and the brow of the quarry on the skyline beyond. Established by associates of Saint Seiriol who dwelt on the island, the original priory was apparently ravaged by the Vikings in the tenth century. The present ruined buildings were the southern part of the cloisters built in the thirteenth century and the Church of Saint Seiriol dates from the same period. The two were joined by the Priory building itself that was built in the sixteenth century and which is today a private residence. The dovecote was erected about 1600 to provide dainty morsels for the table of Sir Richard Bulkeley, the local landowner.

Following the path upwards from the Priory towards Trwyn Du, this is the first view of Puffin Island seen from the top of the rise. The main channel into this eastern end of the Menai lies between the lighthouse and the rock with its red 'perch' beacon.

Small vessels can also pass to the southward of the island (as shown by Lewis Morris in his chart of 1748 [chart 5]) but there is considerably less depth of water on that route. That early chart already showed a perch on the rock, called Carreg Edwen or 'The Horse', but it was a century or so later before the lighthouse was erected on Trwyn Du. While *Trwyn* literally means 'nose' a reasonable translation would be 'Black Point' or perhaps 'Black Naze'.

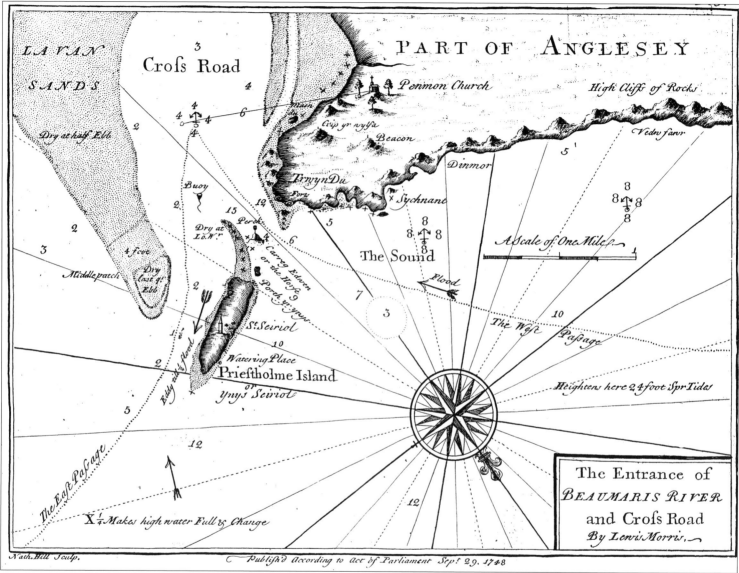

PART OF ANGLESEY

LAVAN SANDS

Cross Road

Dry at half Ebb

3

4

4 4 6

4 4

4

2

Buoy

2

15 12

2

Perok.

2

Middle patch

4 foot

Dry at Lo.Wr.

4

6

Carry Edwen or the Hose Porth yr ynys

Dry last qr Ebb

2

Eddy att ye Flood

St Seiriol

Watering Place

10

Priestholme Island or Ynys Seiriol

The East Passage

5

12

X¼ Makes high water Full & Change

Penmon Church

High Cliff of Rocks

Main

Cvip yr wylfa

Beacon

Vedw farr

TrwynDu

Fort

Dinmor

Sychnant

5

5

8 8 8 8

The Sound

5

8 8 8 8 8

7

Flood

3

A Scale of One Mile.

10

The West Passage

10

Heightens here 24 foot Spr Tides

12

The Entrance of
BEAUMARIS RIVER
and Cross Road
By Lewis Morris.

Nath. Hill Sculp.

Publish'd According to Act of Parliament Sepr. 29. 1748

Chart 5.

102

A small cave in the limestone strata of which the Penmon promontory is formed.

The stony foreshore on the northern side of Trwyn Du. The whole of this eastern corner of Anglesey, from Bwrdd Arthur (Arthur's Table) to the point itself, and also the island, is formed of this carboniferous limestone – as evidenced by the numerous quarries. Wave action results in the limestone cobbles on the beach reducing in size from high water downwards towards the sea.

Trwyn Du Lighthouse at Penmon. (*Pen* can mean 'end' or 'extremity' as well as 'head' while the *mon* is clearly from *Môn*, Anglesey.)

The usual description is 'Penmon Light' though strictly it is Trwyn Du Light as that is the geographical name of the site. It marks the narrow entrance into the Menai which lies between the rock on which the lighthouse is built and the outcrop on the island side of the channel on which the red perch is sited.

The relevant section of Admiralty Chart 1464 'Menai Strait' (reproduced on page 106 as chart 6) shows the light's characteristics abbreviated as follows:

Fl 5 s. 19m 15M

Bell (1) 30s.

To the mariner, these letters and figures indicate: first, that the light flashes every five seconds, then that it is a white light (because there is no symbol indicating to the contrary), next that the lantern is nineteen metres above sea level (at high water) and finally that the light is visible for fifteen miles (to an observer fifteen feet above sea level). In addition to the light there is a bell which strikes once every 30 seconds.

The photograph was taken at low water of a big spring tide when the sea drops to its lowest level.

On the right hand side of the uppermost white band can be seen some letters – and the whole legend can be seen in the photograph on the next page (though too small to read). The full wording is **No Passage Landward** and is imperative advice to any stranger approaching the Strait not to pass inshore of the lighthouse – where the height of the tide hides the rocks from view for much of the time.

The view from the bridge of the *Balmoral* outward bound from the Strait. The lighthouse on the port (left) hand, and the red perch on the starboard (right) hand. From the note on page 27 it will be recalled that red buoys (or beacons) are left to starboard when heading seaward.

The buildings seen on the left of the upper photograph were at one time the local station and accommodation for the Coastguard. Today virtually all the watchkeeping is conducted at the Coastguard headquarters in Holyhead following the great change in communications equipment and practices. Previously, coastal surveillance was maintained visually by a chain of Coastguard stations from where observers covered the sector within their line of sight; nowadays however, almost all vessels have VHF radio which allows a central listening watch covering a very wide area. Independent of weather, visibility, daylight and distance, any of which could limit the result of visual observation, there is no doubting the greater scope provided by radio coverage.

It may be of interest to consider the term 'watch' in this context. It was originally associated with observation by eye, later by telescope, but still retaining the sense of seeing. However, it became such a part of the English language that its meaning was transferred to the radio process as well and today we speak of keeping a 'listening watch' even though the *seeing* has been replaced by *hearing*.

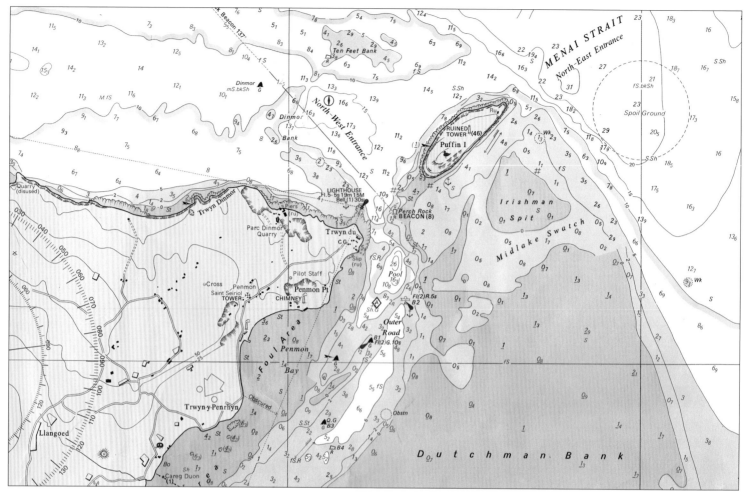

Chart 6. Part of Admiralty Chart 1464 'Menai Strait'.

The eastern end of the Menai at low water of a big spring tide – looking southwest from Puffin Island.

Referring first to chart 5 (page 102) because its orientation is similar to that of the photograph, the channel on the right, between Trwyn Du and the perch is noted as the West Passage while the channel on the left in the photograph is noted as the East Passage. In the modern chart (page 106) they are described as 'North-West Entrance' and 'North-East Entrance' respectively. The photograph also shows the rocky reef extending to the base of the lighthouse, which explains the need for the warning notice discussed on page 104.

The landing beach on the southern side of the island, and the clear strata of its rock formation. There is reference to the religious settlement having been established by Saint Seiriol in the sixth century and the remains of monastic buildings dating from the thirteenth century suggest that the settlement lasted for some centuries.

Known to the Welsh as Ynys Seiriol, its original English name was 'Priestholme' but its most common description today is 'Puffin Island' because of its sea bird population. Early summer sees puffins and guillemots in residence, while gulls, cormorants, shags and other sea birds are also regular visitors.

The southern face again but the eastern end, showing the nature of the cliffs which provide shelter for the hundreds of birds. The sea happens to be absolutely calm, with no whisper of breeze – but it is not always like this! On the contrary the position is extremely exposed and the nearby waters and banks have seen a number of noteworthy shipwrecks.

The northeasterly aspect of the island showing the ruin of the old telegraph station. For some years during the nineteenth century, a visual telegraph service was maintained between Holyhead and Liverpool to pass news and information about shipping movements, particularly the arrival of vessels. The system comprised a chain of signal stations which transmitted messages from one to another by means of a semaphore. This station on Puffin Island was in communication with a similar station at Mynydd Eilian in northeast Anglesey and, in the other direction, with the station on the Great Orme's Head. The service came to an end with the introduction of the electric telegraph in the 1860s. Many of the signal stations were sited in remote spots as they obviously needed height and a clear field of view, but this one on Puffin Island was undoubtedly the most lonely and remote of all.

The island attracts seals as well as birds – here are half a dozen dozing at low water.

The island from the northeast

Having left Puffin astern you may head for Liverpool, Conwy, Holyhead or the Isle of Man – but it will be difficult to find a more attractive waterway, and you're sure to be back!

ACKNOWLEDGEMENTS

It would be impossible to name all those individuals, authors, friends and family members who, directly or indirectly, have contributed to the content of this book. Having absorbed their information and knowledge over a period of some years, I can only thank them most sincerely and trust that this presentation will not impair their own appreciation of the Menai.

Though the thought of this volume had been with me for a long time previously, I had not really done anything constructive about it until I raised the subject with my friend Terry Beggs. At that particular time he had just completed a photographic course at the University of Wales, Bangor and expressed a willingness to undertake the photography required by the project. I can only express my thanks to him for both his excellent camera work and for his ready co-operation. In his turn, Terry is anxious to acknowledge the encouragement and guidance of Glyn Davies who had been his course tutor. I venture also to thank his wife Shirley for her contribution, and for her patience with a husband who adopted unsocial hours in accordance with the vagaries of weather, tides and visibility.

Thanks to Gomer Press for accepting the efforts of two amateurs in the field and particularly to Gari Lloyd and Doug Jones in the compositors' section who dealt so well with the raw material (and who managed to read my handwriting!) – and of course to Bethan Mair and her co-editor, Ceri Wyn Jones, for their direction, advice and friendship.

Within my family, I am grateful to my daughter Sian for her views on the written sections and my grandson David for his 'computer literacy'. More than to anyone however, my thanks go to my wife Eira – without her the book would not have seen the light of day.

The eastern entrance of the Menai and Liverpool Bay.

© Imray